Lose 20 Lbs For Your Wedding Day

Have the Body You Want In 6 Weeks or Less

Melinda Rolf

Contents

Introduction

So you did it! You said yes to the question and have set the date. First of all, let me say "Congratulations" to both you and your fiancé. You have a lot of planning to do but hopefully there is plenty of time. The venue, the reception, the flowers, the dress, the photos, the honeymoon! You are probably spending a boatload of money on this fabulous event and all eyes will be on you. So you want to look and feel your very best. But if that *is* an issue for you, and the fact that you bought this book, tell me that it may be, then don't worry. I can promise you that if you read this book and follow the guidelines you WILL lose at least 20lbs (and possibly much more) by the time the big day comes along.

Sometimes the bride to be will (in a desperate effort) resort to fad diets, pills, and quick fixes. And while these may work and you may lose a few pounds before the big day, chances are you will have gained them back before the Honeymoon is over and you don't want that to happen before he has even carried you over the threshold

In fact, many studies show that marriage itself tends to pack on the pounds, so wouldn't you rather make a smart, reasonable and sustainable change to your diet right now which will in turn lead you staying slim and more importantly, healthier for all those upcoming wedding anniversaries?

And yes, it is a stressful time, which if not checked, can lead to even more weight gain which is the last thing you want right now. But don't despair, it is very possible with the help of this book to start and maintain a healthy diet and fitness regimen. How do you this? Simple! Commit to your plan. Choose to stay in control, one day at a time, no matter what life and wedding planners may throw at you

Besides, there is no such thing as a "one size fits all when it comes to losing weight. There are a million diet books out there that will promise you that if you "Do this, eat this, don't eat that, you will lose X amount of weight in a specific time. But the truth of the matter is, every body is different and what works for one, may not work for another. I don't know you, I don't know your lifestyle, where you work or how you spend your free time. One thing I do know though is that if you read this book and then start to implement the suggestion that I have written, you will lose at least 20lbs in a time frame of about 6 weeks. You may lose it much quicker or perhaps a little slower. But you WILL without a doubt lose weight and inches. This book will teach everything you need to know about the following:

- factors affecting weight

- how to effectively lose weight fast

- what is detoxification

- how to detoxify properly

- what foods to avoid

- what foods to include

- what exercises to perform

And so much more.

This book will guide you through a six week period to achieving desirable weight safely.

Read this book today and see your body transform into a fit, slim and healthy one, and you will be absolutely glowing on your wedding day.

Preparing for Detox by Understanding What It Is All About

Losing weight is more successful when started the right way. It is very important to understand that toxin overload in the body contributes to weight gain. It also interferes with weight loss, making it difficult for the body to effectively metabolize fat. Detoxing is the most important first step to effectively and quickly lose weight. It is also important to understand that to lose weight healthily, your body must first be primed and ready. You have to get rid of all the bad stuff, before you start adding all the good stuff. This is where detoxing comes in.

What is Detox?

Detox is short for detoxification. It is a natural process within the body designed to clean the body. The toxins are processed, modified into non-harmful chemicals and tagged for excretion. Toxins are always in the body. They come from food, from exposure to environmental chemicals and from the body's own natural chemical and metabolic processes. This is why the body has its excretory system designed to remove the waste daily and prevents it from accumulating. Detox described in this book is about helping the body improve its ability to deal with toxins.

This process is not about deprivation, like most people think. Detoxing is not about not eating. It's all about getting rid of the accumulated toxins within the tissues. If not removed, these toxins will trigger a protective reaction.

Toxins are harmful to the body. Over time, the body has no recourse but to protect itself. Protective mechanisms like inflammation and increased fat accumulation happens. The immune system releases inflammatory chemicals and cells. As long as the toxins are still within the tissues, inflammatory cascade continues leading to chronic inflammation.

Fat metabolism is also part of the protective mechanism triggered by the presence of toxins. Chronic inflammation from the above described condition also triggers and stimulates fat storage. Fats are like cushions, which serve to protect the organs from damage. Toxins are threats to the organs because in the presence of toxins, the body increases its fat production to "cover" the organs and protect them from damage. The more toxins in the body, the bigger the threat, and the larger the amount of fats are produced.

Traditional detox methods do incorporate some form of fasting, drinking liquids only and eating weird food. However, this all depends on what kind of detox is done and for what reason.

Why Detox?

Detox is very important, especially for people who want to lose weight. The top reasons for undergoing detox include:

Not feeling well

If the body feels tired the moment you wake up in the morning, it is one sure sign that a detox is a must. Waking up in the morning should make you feel vibrant, alive, energetic, and joyful. But some may find themselves barely having the energy to get out of bed. They walk around like zombies, lazy and unable to focus. Even in the mid hours of the morning, there is already fatigue. The muscles are aching, even though little physical exertion has been made. Discomforts like frequent headaches, allergies and digestive concerns like gas, bloating, constipation and diarrhea. All these problems are not related to any illness or infection, and are often unresponsive to common medications. It's amazing that once detox is done, all these will be gone, without any drugs.

Difficulty losing or maintaining ideal weight

This is a common problem, not only among those who actively try to lose weight but the general population as well. First off, forget about the greatest myth in weight loss that eating less calories will keep the weight off. Weight gain or loss is not just about counting calories. It is more complex than that. One of the major contributing factors to weight gain and difficulty losing excess weight is the presence of toxins in the body. These toxins come from everywhere, food, water, medications, personal care products, and even from the body's own natural metabolic processes. The body has means to get rid of the toxins that inevitably enter or form within the body. There is the liver, kidneys and other excretory organs like the skin, lungs and colon.

The accumulated toxins in the body promote more fat production and inhibit fat burning. They trigger the body's protective mechanism and immune response, which triggers the fat producing hormones and processes. Detoxing removes the accumulated toxins and allows the body to restart, to breathe and return to normal function. That includes giving the body's natural fat burning mechanism to kick in and promote natural and fast weight loss.

Cravings

Cravings are uncontrollable, insistent urge to eat certain foods. The urge to eat is no necessarily due to real hunger. And as you follow the cravings, the more calories are consumed leading to weight gain. Also, these cravings make it difficult to follow a healthier diet and maintain optimum weight.

Unhealthy cravings are for sugar and carbs such as those made with white or refined flour. These foods are considered as addictive foods. They trigger a cycle that feeds itself and intensifie over time. It becomes worse as you keep feeding the cravings.

Detoxing helps flush the toxins produced by sugar and flour. It resets the system, which is th only plausible way to stop the cravings. Years of eating tons of sugar and flour has caused the system to deviate from its normal rhythm and function. By detoxing, the body gets the much needed reset i order to return to its normal, efficient process.

Sugar, in particular, is a highly addictive substance. It is actually more addictive than the dru cocaine. In fact, a few experts consider sugar as the new nicotine- highly addictive, widely available and difficult to stay away from. One huge food industry secret is that sugar in most foods is heavil modified in order to stimulate what insiders call the "bliss point". This is what promotes a sense o satisfaction when eating junk foods that are full of sugar. Ever found yourself munching on a huge ba of cookies or chips in just one sitting and then you find yourself reaching for another? Try eating bowl of fruit and you won't be reaching for another one right after. The difference is in the type o sugar content. Sugar in store-bought cookies is very different from sugar in fruits. Sugar in thes commercial foods is refined, which means it is modified or altered. The alterations were specificall designed, i.e., chemically altered so that when consumed, it will modify the body's set point for suga It will also trigger "heavy use" (tolerance for huge consumption) and increases "stomach share (capacity to consume more and to delay feelings of fullness despite having eaten a lot).

Proper Detox Guidelines

The first thing to understand is that detox helps the body be more efficient in cleaning itself.

will not flush out 100% of all the toxins in the body. The entire process is all about how to avoid adding more to the body's toxin load. By easing up on the daily toxins that gets added into the tissues, the liver gets to function better. Just think of detox as giving the timeout by avoiding all known toxin sources. This way, the body can focus its energies into cleaning up itself. If toxins keep adding up, the body will keep trying to catch up with the work and try to deal with current toxins. The past toxins will be set aside, left to circulate in the body and eventually ending up within the tissues. If the liver is not currently preoccupied with incoming toxins, it can concentrate on dealing with previous toxins, metabolizing and tagging them for excretion. Think of a person with a desk job, dealing with paperwork. Every day, new piles of papers come to his desk, which he must sort out, separating the waste papers and the ones that are still needed. Imagine if every day, he receives more than what he is normally capable of. He probably won't be able to sort out all of it at the end of the day. The worst part is, most of the load is waste paper anyways. The next day, when he receives a new batch of paperwork, he puts it on top of the previous day's and tries to deal with today's. If he finishes early, he can continue sorting the ones from the previous day. But, if the work load is always more than he can handle, he'll soon find himself buried in a mountain of paper. And this mountain of paper slows him down even more, worsening his predicament. The best way to deal with this problem is to minimize the daily work load. This way, he can efficiently handle the day's requirements and still have enough time to process the accumulated paper works from previous days. This is what happens to the liver when you are constantly exposed to toxins. Detoxing is giving the liver less workload for a few days in order to give it a chance to process backlog of toxins and other compounds in the body.

There are 3 main ways to detox properly. These are:

1.Reduce exposure to toxins (from both environmental sources and from food)

2.Consume foods that promote, support or stimulate the natural detoxification process

3.Adapt a lifestyle that sustains minimal toxin exposure and maximizes proper body function, especially natural detoxification process

Basically, these steps promote three basic things. First, they promote the movement of toxins from within the tissues where they are stored. The toxins are mostly stored within the fatty layers that surround the various tissues in the body. Next, the mobilized toxins enter the blood stream and are brought to the liver for detoxification. Some are brought to the kidneys for direct excretion.

Toxins brought to the liver are processed into non-harmful forms and then tagged before they are brought back into circulation. These tags mark the toxins to be delivered to the colon and the kidneys for excretion. The tags are very important so that the toxins will not go back and be stored in the fats and tissues. Finally, the toxins are in water soluble form and excreted via the urine or feces.

Every step is important. But the most crucial step is the second one, when the toxins enter the liver and are processed. Detox should support this critical step in order to be successful at removing toxins and promoting health and optimum weight loss.

Reduce Exposure to Environmental Toxins

Today's environment is filled with toxins, from the air, water and even from land. Controlling the toxins in the environment requires massive, collective effort form the entire society. And it will take decades to clean up the toxins in the environment. In the meantime, you can do something to limit your exposure to these harmful chemicals.

Fewer Pollutants in the Home

Most people think of urban or industrial areas as the only place where they can get exposed to tons of pollutants. Surprisingly, the home is also full of toxins. Where do they come from? Household chemicals like dishwashing liquids, cleaning solutions, air fresheners, bleach, laundry detergents, antimicrobial solutions and other similar products. Anything that comes in a bottle is most likely a concoction of chemicals that can be sources of toxins. These artificial chemicals can leave residue over different surfaces. When skin or food comes into contact with the contaminated surfaces, the chemical residues will enter the body. For example, dishwashing liquid leave soap and chemical residues on utensils, kitchen appliances, plates, food containers, spoon, fork, etc. When these are used to prepare food, the residue will mix with the food. When eaten, these residues enter the body and cause problems, including fat accumulation and difficulty losing excess weight.

So, instead of using these chemical household products, use natural cleaners. White vinegar mixed with water is a safer all-around cleaner. It's natural, cleans effectively and does not leave any chemical residue. Another alternative is making a thick paste with baking soda and a little water. This effectively cuts grease and leaves surface clean, smelling fresh and looking shiny without any residue.

Some use air fresheners to improve the smell inside the house. Toxins from the chemical in air fresheners, sprays and perfumes get inhaled. In the lungs, it can promote respiratory problems. Remove all of these to lessen the exposure to pollutants.

Dry cleaning is also a source of toxins. Potent chemicals are used to remove stains, smell and to make clothes look clean and like new. These chemicals are also toxic and can enter the body through inhalation.

Reduce Exposure to Food Toxins

Toxins can also come from foods. Processed foods are the main sources of toxins because of the many artificial chemicals and the various processes that raw food materials undergo. All these create compounds that can be bad for health. Processed foods are not just the usual junk foods we know. There are also "disguised" junk foods. Some people think that just because the foods come with "healthy" labels they no longer pose any health risk. Some of these contain potentially harmful compounds or compounds that can stimulate unhealthy processes in the body.

Foods Labeled "Fat-Free" and "Low Fat"

Saturated fats have been cast in a bad light in recent years. These were labeled as bad fats that cause people to gain excess weight and develop health problems like diabetes, obesity and cardiovascular diseases. And in response to this, products that boast of being "fat-free" or "low fat". People now think that these labels mean that the product is healthy. Well, it's not. When fat is removed from food, the taste turns horrible. To improve taste, tons of sugars are added. So, the food may be fat-free but it's full of sugar, which is a more dangerous chemical than fat. In fact, the body has more use for saturated fat compared to the sugar used in these low-fat and fat-free foods. Hence, these foods are actually more junk and harmful to health than foods with natural fats in them.

Commercial Salad Dressings

Vegetables and salads are healthy, but the dressing may not be. Most vegetables do not taste great on their own and dressings can greatly improve their palatability. However, most commercial dressings are loaded with unhealthy ingredients such as sugars, trans fats and unhealthy vegetable oils. There are also a bunch of other artificial chemicals added to improve taste, stabilize the consistency of the dressing and to prolong its shelf life. Sometimes, food colors are also added to make the dressing look appealingly vibrant. Using these commercial dressings can offset the healthy benefits that can be obtained from the vegetables. More so if the dressing comes labeled as "fat-free" or "low-fat".

Fruit Juices

Fruits are healthy but fruit juices are not, even when they are made fresh and from whole, organic fruits. Fruit juices are essentially liquid sugar. Fruit juices from fresh and organic fruits are concentrated natural sugars. Even if it's natural, the high concentration can still cause a few health problems. It can get converted into fat and stored. Also, fruit juices do not contain any of the nutrients found in real, whole fruits such as most of the vitamins, fiber and minerals. So, it's basically pure liquid sugar, which is unhealthy in large concentrations

Commercial fruit juices are even worse. Most of these do not even contain any actual fruit or juice from fruits. These are mostly flavored liquids. Artificial chemicals are added to make the mixture taste like fruit, with tons of sugar poured in to make it taste sweet and delicious.

Whole Wheat Products

Whole wheat is deemed as healthy food for the heart. It is rich in fiber that soaks up and absorbs toxins as well as excess fats, making these ready for excretion. However, products that are labeled "whole wheat" are not always the same as the real whole wheat. Most of these whole wheat products contain grains that have been pulverized, turned into flour. While the grain may be whole wheat, it was processed and heavily broken down. Its effects in the body will still be the same as white or refined flour. It can quickly raise the blood sugar level and set off fat accumulation and rapid weight gain, along with associated health issues like obesity and diabetes. Studies have found that bread made from whole wheat flour has the same glycemic index as white bread (bread made from white or refined flour). Glycemic index refers to how fast a food product or item increases the blood sugar levels after consumption.

Another issue is that wheat cultivated today is already very much different from the original wheat crop decades ago. It has already been genetically modified through the years to make it yield more harvest and be hardier against pests, drought and other environmental factors that often damage wheat crops. Hence, it is no longer reliable to provide the original health benefits obtained from the unaltered wheat of the past generations. Today's wheat is already less nutritious. It is also richer in gluten, which can initiate symptoms in people with gluten sensitivity or intolerance. A few studies have even found links between today's wheat and whole wheat products to the development of inflammatory conditions in the body as well as increase in the levels of cholesterol. Hence, it's best to avoid wheat altogether because it is no longer the same as the wheat that is originally heart-healthy.

13

Phytosterols

Phytosterols are essentially the plant version of cholesterol found in animals. These are natur plant compounds claimed to reduce the levels of cholesterol in the body. Because of this effec phytosterols are often added in most "healthy" foods. However, despite this cholesterol-lowerir effect, it can have adverse effects on the heart and the rest of the cardiovascular system. In som people, the risk for heart diseases and death are increased with the consumption of phytosterols.

Margarine

This is promoted by some as a healthier alternative to butter. Back in the day, butter wa discouraged because of the high amount of saturated fat it contains. However, the alternativ margarine contains high amounts of trans fats, which are more dangerous to health than saturate fats. Today's margarine has less trans fats due to the increased awareness about the negative effec of trans fats. However, it still contains refined vegetable oils that are bad for health.

Margarine is essentially not food. It is an artificial food product created from an assembly different refined oils and chemicals. It has gone various processes in order to make it look and tast like food. Hence, it is not real and essentially junk food. It lacks any useful nutrients because it essentially artificial. Another concern is that the more processes, the less nutritious, the worse th effects are in the body.

The irony about using margarine is that it was promoted as a healthier alternative to butter. study found that people who used margarine in place of butter actually had higher risks fo cardiovascular problems. They also have higher probabilities of dying from heart diseases. Consumir fully artificial, trans fat-rich margarine is so much worse than real butter.

Sports Drinks

Originally, sports drinks were formulated for athletes. These were supposed to replenish th electrolytes and glucose lost from sweating during training and sports activities. Athletes do benefit lot from sports drinks because the sugar and salt (electrolytes are easily absorbed in their bodie quickly replenishing what was lost. These sports drinks are only meant to be a tempora replenishment. Essentially, the athlete will quickly burn the liquid sugar, leaving very little chance be converted into fats or to wreak imbalance in the body.

However, these sports drinks are not meant to be consumed by people not engaged in activities that involve sweating a lot. Regular activities would not require additional salts and sugar from these sports drinks. Again, added sugars are not good for health.

Some people think that sports drinks are better than sugar-rich soft drinks. The only difference is that sports drinks have slightly lower sugar contents compared to soft drinks, but the negative effects are relatively the same.

Hydration is very important, regardless if engaged in regular physical activities or strenuous exercises. Water is still the best. The only reason why sports drinks are popular among athletes is to help prevent problems like low blood sugar and muscle cramps while they are engaged in sports that usually last long. For example, an athlete competing in basketball, which would last for more than an hour would lose electrolytes through sweat. Sugar in the body is quickly burned to provide energy to the muscles. If the body has to depend on natural processes to replenish the sugar and electrolytes, the athlete would soon find himself in trouble, suffering from hypoglycemia (low blood sugar levels) which could lead to weakness and even fainting. Low electrolyte levels can lead to problems like muscle cramps. Sports drinks are meant to be temporary replenishment to prevent these. Also, quick electrolyte and glucose replacement improves the athlete's endurance, helping to last longer into the game and to maintain top performance. But for people who are into less than an hour of physical exertion like regular exercise, water is still the best way to keep hydrated. The body can supply the needed electrolytes and sugar needs under regular types of physical activities.

Low Carbohydrate Junk Foods

Carbohydrates, like fats, have been cast in a negative light. A lot of people think that all carbohydrates get converted into fats. Going on a low carbohydrate diet does help in losing weight. It can also help in improving one's health. Manufacturers took advantage of the growing interest in weight loss through low carb diets. They created low carb versions of their processed, junk foods. Everything came in low-carb versions- low-carb boxed cereals, low-carb dressings, low-carb cookies, low-carb food bars etc. All these are supposedly enough to help one lose weight. This made people think that just because it's low-carb, it's supposedly healthy. Not quite so.

Check the ingredients list at the back of these processed foods. It's a list of hard-to-read chemicals and refined ingredients. Yes, it's low carb because it does not contain any real food that

15

does contain carbohydrates. There aren't any real nutrients that the body can use.

Agave Nectar

This is offered as an alternative to sugar, particularly white refined sugar. Agave nectar is marketed as a natural sweetener that does not cause the same negative effects as white sugar. This belief led to its use as a sweetener in a lot of "health foods". On closer inspection, agave syrup can be much worse than white sugar. The problem with refined white sugar is its high fructose content. Fructose, frequently consumed in large amounts causes metabolic imbalances that lead to the development of problems like diabetes. White sugar, on the average, contains 50% fructose. High fructose corn syrup (HFCS), a common and very dangerous type of sugar, contains about 55% of fructose. Agave nectar, or agave syrup, deemed to be a healthier alternative, contains so much more. It contains about 70 to 90% fructose. So much for being "healthy".

Vegan Junk Foods

Vegan diets are increasingly becoming more popular. The increasing awareness on health is one of the driving forces for its popularity. And with this growing awareness, manufacturers are again jumping into the bandwagon. There are now vegan substitutes for meat and meat-based products. For instance, vegan bacon is becoming very popular. While true that these products may not have any dairy, poultry or meat ingredients, these are still highly processed foods. The flavorings that make these vegan substitutes tasty are full of processed ingredients, along with lots of sugar, flour and salt.

Brown Rice Syrup

This is also known as rice malt syrup. This is among the claimed "natural" sweeteners that can substitute for white refined sugar. This is mistakenly considered as healthy. Like other similar products, natural does not always mean healthy.

Brown rice syrup is produced by adding enzymes to cooked rice. These enzymes break down the starch in rice. This breakdown converts the starch in rice into simple sugars, which is now known as brown rice syrup. These simple sugars are purely glucose. There is no refined fructose in this product, which at first may be good. However, brown rice syrup has high glycemic index, which is 98. Glucose in this syrup raises blood sugar levels rapidly.

Another concern about brown rice syrup is that it is highly refined. It contains very little, almost negligible, amount of nutrients. It's nothing more than just pure liquid sugar and nothing else. It only provides large amounts of calories but is considered as empty calories because the body has no real use for it. There is also a growing concern on the risk for arsenic poisoning associated with the use of this sweetener.

Processed Organic Foods

Not all organic foods are healthy. The raw food may come from organic sources but underwent several manufacturing processes that it no longer resembles whole, healthy, organic food. These foods have been altered that it is no longer different from other processed foods. It is the same junk, even if it used organic food as a raw ingredient.

Processed foods that boast of being organic are usually ones that contain organic ingredients such as organic raw cane sugar. This ingredient may be organic but in not necessarily healthy. It is 100% similar to regular, white refined sugar, with the same unhealthy effects on the body. It's just fructose and glucose, with no other nutrients.

Vegetable Oils

Vegetable oils, along with seed oils are advised to be healthier alternative. Studies show that these have cholesterol-lowering Studies have also shown that consuming vegetable oils can increase a person's risk of dying from cancer and heart diseases. The mere reduction of cholesterol is not enough to lower one's risk for health problems like stroke and heart attacks. Hence, it is still not advisable to consume vegetable oils on a daily basis.

Another note on vegetable oils is that these are refined foods. And again, refined foods have been so heavily altered that they lack substantial nutrients. It's still better to use natural fats that are much healthier. Examples include olive oil, butter and coconut oil.

Processed Gluten-Free Foods

A growing portion of the population is actively avoiding gluten. This is another "health" and "diet" trend that may be more harmful when improperly done. First off, avoiding gluten is only medically advisable to people who suffer from some form of sensitivity or intolerance to gluten. This is a protein found in grains like wheat, triticale, barley and rye. People who are intolerant or sensitive to gluten experience discomforts like gastrointestinal upset, weight loss and nutritional deficiencies.

In some people, going gluten-free can help in detoxifying the body and to some extent, weight loss. However, processed food labeled as gluten-free is not always healthy. It is still processed and unhealthy. These may have taken out the gluten but that also includes much of the nutrients. It is essentially nutrient-deficient. These processed gluten-free foods are also high in refined flours, which cause rapid spikes in the levels of glucose in the blood. Also, not everything labeled "gluten-free" is really free form all traces of gluten. This protein can come in different forms, such as the ingredients used for flavoring, preserving, stabilizing or coloring the food.

Processed Breakfast Cereals

Marketing strategies for breakfast cereals make these products appear healthy. Things like "low fat" and "whole grain" mislead people into thinking that these can provide the body's energy needs for the day while keeping them healthy and helping them lose weight. Browse the ingredients list at the back of the cereal box and see that there is very little real food. It's just artificial chemicals (for flavor, coloring, etc.) and refined grain and sugar.

So now that you know how to prepare your body for healthy weight s by detoxing first, you are now ready to begin. Are you ready? Let's get started

HINT

When eating, do nothing else. Turn off the TV, your phone or laptop and just eat. When you concentrate on the food you are eating the flavor and enjoyment will be so much more intense. You will find yourself more full and satisfied, and less likely to want to reach for that bag of cookies mid-day. But if you do find yourself craving chocolate, try a square of Lindt dark. With only 40 calories per square, this will take the edge off your craving. And dark chocolate has other health properties too.

Taking Body Measurements

Taking body measurements is very important to establish current weight status and what goals should be made. This also helps to track progress with weight loss regimen.

A tape measure is used when taking body measurements. The following body parts are measured and recorded. Changes in the values obtained reflect the progress towards weight loss:

- shoulders
- neck
- chest
- biceps
- waist
- hips
- thighs

Waist to Hip Ratio

Examples of body measurements that help determine health status is the hip-to-waist ratio. This reflects if central obesity is present or if a person is at risk for it. It also helps to determine body shape and in determining BMI.

To measure, the World Health Organization (WHO) tells to take the waist circumference at the midpoint from the margin of the last rib (palpable rib) to the top of the iliac crest (pointy hip bones). The hip circumference is obtained by taking the circumference at the level of the widest part of the buttocks. When taking measurements, stand straight, with the feet closed next to each other. The arms should be relaxed at the sides. Take measurements after you exhale.

People with higher waist circumferences than the hip are said to have apple-shaped bodies. These people have higher risks for developing health problems like hormonal imbalance, diabetes, heart diseases and stroke among others. People with higher hip circumference are said to have pear-shaped bodies, with lower risk than apple-shaped bodies.

Starting a Food Log

A food log is a daily entry of what was eaten for the day. It also includes everything that was taken in, such as how many glasses of water, what other beverages were taken such as tea or coffee, how many cups and, if applicable, alcohol. Included are activities for the day. A food log also contains the person's emotions and thoughts, as well as physical reactions to food. For example,

- 9 AM: breakfast with cereals and yogurt. Felt full and energized.

- 9:30 AM: Drove to work.

- 10 AM: At work, felt sluggish. Cravings for sweet food.

- 10:15 AM: Ate chocolate bar, fun-sized

The goal of a food log is to monitor what was eaten, what triggered hunger cues and how the body reacted. This is helpful when trying to lose weight or when trying to detect any food allergies or intolerances. This is also helpful in identifying what triggers cravings or overeating. For example, upon reviewing the food log, a person found that prior to eating an entire tub of ice cream, stress at work was too great. Or, the mid-morning low energy and intense cravings for sweets was due to a breakfast meal of bad carbohydrates.

A food log also helps when tracking calorie consumption, weight differences and food expenditures. This is where a record of everything related to food and weight can be recorded for later evaluation. A food log is important to keep track of what techniques were effective and which ones are not.

Track your "tastings". During this time you will find yourself sampling lots of wedding cake, soups for your reception. Hopefully this will be over a period of time and not on the same day. But whenever it is, be sure to record every bite as those calories can soon add up.

Creating a Daily Eating Plan

A daily eating plan is a written plan of what to eat. This is very important to keep within a diet. An eating plan helps to reduce the stress of having to think of what to eat at each meal. This also reduces the risk of just ordering unhealthy take out or reaching for a bag of processed chips and other unhealthy processed foods.

A daily meal should consist of the following, at least:......

- 5 servings of vegetables and fruits, about ½ cup

- 9 servings of whole grain rice, cereal or pasta, which is about ½ cup or equivalent to a slice of bread

- 8 ounces of poultry, lean meat, fish or any non-meat equivalent of protein. Servings are any of the following:

  □ ½ cup of beans

  □ 1 ounce of meat-based 2-3 ounces of tofu

  □ 1 medium-sized egg

- 3 servings of cottage cheese, yogurt or low-fat milk, about 1 cup

Always Eat Breakfast.

Breakfast is an easy meal to prepare and can get you ready for the busy day ahead. Be sure to eat a healthy breakfast every morning. This will get your metabolism going which will help you make healthier choices throughout the day. Studies have shown that those that eat a healthy breakfast are more likely to lose weight than those who skip. So be sure to start off your day the correct way.

HINT: Always Have Healthy Snacks at Hand.

This is a very busy time and much of it will be spent rushing around. There is not always time to stop and eat something healthy so always have some healthy snacks in your bag or car. This will help you avoid the possibility of the fast food drive through, which is a disastrous move for anyone trying to lose weight and get healthier.

Weighing Guidelines

When weighing, one has to follow a few guidelines in order to get accurate readings.

- Weigh in the morning. The most preferred time is before eating breakfast, after urinating. At this time, the body is well rested and not bloated or swollen from activities.

- Weigh using the same scale each day.

- Use minimal amount of clothing when weighing. If possible, use the same clothes for weighing such as a robe each day.

- When weighing, avoid moving around too much.

- Do not lean forward when looking at the readings. This can cause inaccurate readings.

- Weigh at the same time each day. Weight readings tend to differ at different times of the day. For example, some women tend to weigh a bit more when taking weight measurement at noon or later in the day.

- If possible, have the weighing scale in the same area, in the same room. Avoid weighing in different areas of the house.

- Always record daily readings to serve as monitoring and evaluation tools for the effectiveness of a chosen method.

Cutting Out Alcohol (At Least until the Reception)

Alcohol is a foreign chemical that can trigger some unhealthy process in the body. In large amounts consumed frequently over a long period, alcohol can cause damage to the liver. This can seriously decrease the body's capability to detoxify itself. Liver damage can also cause more problems with nutrient absorption and fat metabolism.

There are studies that link drinking alcohol in moderation to decreasing risk for cardiovascular diseases. There are also quite a few studies that show red wine as helpful in keeping a slim figure. Studies show that resveratrol in red wine is responsible for these health benefits. Health experts caution people against jumping into wine drinking, especially those who have not been previously drinking wine and other forms of alcohol. Drinking can eventually prove to cause more harm than good.

Also, alcohol also comes with large amounts of calories, empty calories. Think of just how much sugar is added to a small cocktail, with all those added juices and flavors. This adds to the excess fat production and difficulty losing weight. So if you are really serious about losing weight and keeping it off, stop drinking alcohol. (At least until the reception)

HINT

Drink your water.

Recent studies found that when people drink more water throughout the day, they end up eating fewer total calories. Another new study found that drinking water before each meal resulted in greater weight loss. Water and water-rich foods can help fill you up longer. Keep a cup of water in hand at parties, sip water between bites, and meet your daily quota to help prevent overeating.

Exercise is Key

Weight loss and achieving a healthier body requires regular exercise. One has to engage in some level of physical activity to keep organs working and blood flowing properly.

Start With Low Intensity

Start with low intensity, low impact sports or exercise. This is most recommended for people who have not been exercising for quite some time. Low intensity exercises are generally aimed at improving oxygenation and joint movement. It also improves blood circulation.

Walking

Walking is the simplest and very effective form of exercise. It works out all the major muscle groups, promoting enhanced blood flow. Toxins are removed while the metabolism is adequately revved up. It is easy on the joints because it does not require much flexibility.

Start by walking around the block or park, for about 15 to 30 minutes. Walk at a brisk pace, enough to make the respiration quicken but not to the point of running out of breath. Keep it relaxed but still pushing the body a little bit. Weight loss and increased metabolism is brought about by activities that increase respiratory rates and pulse rates. You do not necessarily have to sweat hard just to burn fats and lose weight. So it's not really imperative to start exercising with moderate to heavy workouts. In fact, starting with low intensity is better and has lower risk of injuring yourself. This is especially so among beginners or people who have not been exercising regularly previously.

Try Meditation or Yoga

These are great activities that promote better health. They also help in naturally cleansing the body which can help in speeding up weight loss, although indirectly. By improving blood flow, more oxygen and nutrients reach the cells, which improve function and increases metabolic activities. This effect also promotes the removal of wastes from the tissues and be brought to the liver and kidneys for detoxification and excretion.

Yoga, in particular, is a great form of exercising without taxing the body too much. This is best for people who are too heavy for some exercises or who have issues with joint mobility and/or muscle function. It helps to releases stress while improving health and bodily functions. Yoga also helps a

24

person improve flexibility and balance.

Meditation can be performed alone or while doing yoga exercises. It clears the mind and improves oxygenation. It also helps in relaxing the body. This way, the other tissues and organs function more efficiently because they are not restricted by adjacent tight muscles.

Exercising with Moderate Intensity

Moderate intensity exercises are those that promote physical exertion. These are exercises that will cause you to sweat and breathe heavily. This helps to eliminate more toxins through the sweat. This also promotes faster metabolic rates to burn more of the fat stores in the body. Do this only after the body has already gotten used to exercising. Doing so will reduce the risk for injuries such as strain, sprain and easy muscle fatigue.

Examples of moderate intensity exercises are brisk walking, jogging, running and weight training. This may also include aerobic exercises and some weight lifting.

This type of exercise also often requires joint flexibility and muscle strength. Hence, it is important to start with less resistance and gradually increase it over the next few days. This is to reduce any serious injuries to joints and muscles such as pulled muscles or muscle tears.

Exercising Outdoors

Going outside exposes the body to environmental pollution. Working out is good but where it takes place may do more harm than the benefits obtained from the exercise. Avoid exercising where there is a lot of pollution. That means no walking along busy streets, where you will inhale the exhaust from passing cars. The best place is a suburban area with a few cars, or in parks where the air is fresher.

People in the city may also be better off in timing when to exercise outdoors. In heavily polluted urban areas, the air quality is generally poor during the early mornings and evenings. At these times, the air is dense because the environmental temperature is low. The particulates (pollutants) are suspended in the air. There isn't much circulation because air is dense. This is why most people may find themselves suffering from symptoms of respiratory difficulties at these times. People with asthma and related respiratory conditions should avoid exercising outdoors during these times. As the environmental temperatures rises, air becomes a bit lighter and the particulates in the air rises. This can make breathing easier because the air is no longer laden with pollutants. However in busy urban areas, there are still a considerable amount of pollutants in the air.

In places where pollution is a problem, it is more prudent to exercise indoors. Go to a gym where air is filtered. Indoor exercise should still be comfortable, with adequate ventilation and proper air filters in order to get the most benefits without getting exposed to pollution.

HINT

Look at your time at the gym like any other of the important schedules you have during this time. For instance, you would not miss a cake testing, or a dress fitting would you? So treat your time at the gym as important as these appointments. Add them to your calendar with all your other important dates. It does not have to be the gym, it can be a workout at home, a bike ride or a brisk walk. It doesn't really matter as long as you schedule them and keep to your schedule.

You Have to Manage Your Stress

I don't need to tell you that these few weeks can be quite stressful as so many decisions have to be made and sometimes things do not go as planned. But stress can be your weight loss enemy if you do not keep it under control. So be sure to include some "me time" in your plans . And practice some one minute breathing exercises on a daily basis. Schedule yourself a massage or some extra long baths. And remember, exercise is a terrific stress buster.

HINT

Catch your zzz's. This is going to be an extremely crazy fun time for you and your calendar is probably full of things you need to take care of. Make sure that "GET PLENTY OF SLEEP is on your calendar too. Not enough sleep will absolutely effect your weight-loss efforts in a negative way leading to increasing cravings and poor choices. Staying organized will help, but do your best to stick to a consistent sleep schedule, aiming for at least 7-8 hour hours per night—And yes....that includes weekends. You do not want to be walking down the aisle in the most beautiful dress ever with big dark circles under your eyes.

Healthy Eating Out

During the days up to the wedding there might be occasions where you have to eat out. Living and eating healthy does not mean you have to be a recluse. It does not mean never setting foot in a restaurant. It just means being more vigilant and be more aware of things.

Checking the Menu Beforehand

There are restaurants that post their menu on their websites or social media accounts. Bloggers also provide some information on the menu of some restaurants they've been to. Also, groups and communities like Weight Watchers and other health-conscious groups and online communities can be sources of this information. Join health-related forums, where suggestions on what restaurants cater best to certain health goals. By knowing the menu beforehand, you are prepared on what to order. You get to choose and make smart decisions beforehand. This is also one way avoiding impulsively ordering that decadent chocolate slice that's sure to be made from loads of refined flour and white sugar.

Stay Away From Chips and Bread Baskets

Restaurants often offer bread baskets before they start serving orders. Bread and chips contain the major food items to stay away from- refined flour and refined sugar. It also has gluten. Some may even contain trans-fat and other unhealthy ingredients. Getting this complimentary basket while hungry and waiting for food may make it hard to stay within the diet. Breads are most often from wheat flour and corn chips are from corn. Both of these raw materials (wheat and corn) are hybridized or genetically modified. In simplest terms, these are artificial, although they grow naturally in the land. Food made from these are empty of calories and create imbalance in the body that lead to excess fat production and accumulation, and will make it very difficult to lose weight.

Bring Homemade Dressings and Condiments

Commercial dressings and condiments are full of refined flour, sugar, gluten, trans fats or processed oils (such as corn, canola and soy oils), preservatives, additives and other artificial chemicals. To avoid these when eating out, bring your own homemade dressing or condiment. Learn how to make the healthier version of favorite condiments and dressings and bring them along when eating out. Do not be shy about asking your food to be made and served without the restaurant's condiment and dressings. For example, have salads served without any dressing. Pour your own healthier version, such as vinaigrette made with organic apple cider vinegar and extra virgin olive oil, without the additives, preservatives and other artificial ingredients. Instead of using ketchup or mayonnaise from the restaurant, make your own healthy version using healthy oils and organic eggs without additives, preservatives, stabilizers and all those junk.

Keeping Things Simple

The simpler the meal, the healthier it is. It means less risk that an unhealthy ingredient may have been inadvertently added. Simply prepared meals are those that have been baked, grilled, or any cooking method that used minimal or no oil at all. Also, choose dishes that contain more natural or fresh ingredients such as grilled salmon with fresh salad. Avoid those that are served or cooked in gravies or sauces. Also, it's best to avoid food that has breading in it. Sauces, breading and gravies usually use gluten or flour as thickeners. Also, the seasonings added may also contain some unhealthy ingredients as well. Keep it simple, keep it healthy.

Speak Up

Some people are hesitant to speak up, to ask question or make some special requests when they dine out. They think that if they do, people will misunderstand. Others may treat them as "high maintenance" or too picky. Don't be. Your health should be your first and foremost concern. Besides, there is already a growing awareness on how to be healthy so it's more likely that people will understand your dietary needs.

Gluten-Free Menu

While going gluten-free is not actually recommended for everyone and that it does not directly cause weight loss, most gluten-free foods are healthy. When unable to decide, one of the safe bets is to order from the gluten-free menu. This won't be totally free form any unhealthy ingredients but will surely have minimal additive sin it. Most preservatives, stabilizers, flavorings, thickeners and colorants are all gluten-based, along with other harmful chemicals. By removing all potential gluten sources, a huge load of toxins are also removed from food. Also, no gluten means it does not have any refined flour in it.

Ask for Salads or Vegetables as a Side Dish

Often, side dishes in most restaurants are fried or processed. Examples are fried onion rings, French fries, Belgian fries, corn chips, toast, etc. Request to have vegetables like fresh carrot sticks, sliced fresh cucumbers or celery stalks instead. Another better side dish option is a salad, but without the restaurant's dressings.

Ask What Oil Was Used

Speak up and ask about your food to make sure it was prepared the healthy way. Ask if any oil was used or added to any element in the food. For example, if oil was used in preparing the meat, poultry, fish or vegetables. Also, ask if oil was added to the dressing or condiments. Then, ask what type of oil was used. It is well within your rights to ask what gets into your food because it's your body that suffer the consequences if you are not vigilant enough. Stay away from processed, hydrogenated, trans or refined oils. These include vegetable oils and canola. These contain large amounts of polyunsaturated inflammatory omega-6 fatty acids. These also have low smoking points, which means they easily get burned. When oils get burned, the molecules are altered and harmful compounds are formed.

All these may seem too much work. But with enough knowledge, eating out should be stress-free yet healthy.

HINT

You are going to mess up. It is Inevitable. But don't make a mountain out of a molehill. If you cheat one day, so what? Don't stress about it. Remember, this is a marathon not a sprint so just chalk it up to experience and start the next day as though it was the very first day.

Recognizing Sugar and its Effects

Notice that most of the foods that need to be removed from the diet contain sugar, specifically fructose and refined white sugar. Let's understand exactly what these types of sugar do to the body.

Why the Concern Over Sugar?

These days, people are consuming more sugar than previous generations. On the average, an adult consumes sugar at 64 pounds each year- at least. That would mean eating an average of 22 teaspoons of added sugar each day. An average teen consumes a minimum of 109 pounds of sugar each year. That would mean eating around 34 teaspoons of added sugar per day. Since 1983, the consumption of added sugars per capita has risen by 28%. How can anyone eat so much sugar in a day, in a year? If you mix tea or coffee, you only add about a teaspoon. Where do all these sugars come from? It is hidden in various kinds of foods.

So, what happens if we eat too much sugar?

Sugar in the body causes a lot of problems. First, its immediate effect is on the blood sugar regulatory mechanism. Sugar, particularly fructose and refined sugar, immediately increases the levels of sugar in the blood. These spikes will also rapidly crash because it stimulated a sudden release of large amounts of insulin. This part of the body's regulatory mechanism. But it cannot go on for an extended period without the body suffering seriously. One effect is the development of insulin resistance and diabetes. It also increases the risk for the development of cardiovascular diseases, obesity and metabolic syndrome.

Another effect is that sugar is packed with calories but these are empty calories. These do not provide any nutrition. And yet, it sets off a cycle that feeds itself, creating negative impact on health.

People who consume a lot of sugar also tend to eat less of the nutrients needed by the body. According to a study made by CSPI or Center for Science in the Public Interest, diets high in sugar also tend to be very low in vitamins, fiber and minerals, as well as other necessary nutrients. High sugar diets also tend to displace proteins and other important nutrients that play protective roles in the body. This places a person at higher risk for certain cancers, heart problems, high blood pressure and osteoporosis.

The Issue on "Added Sugars"

Because of the growing concern over the effect of sugar in the body, the USDA and FDA have passed regulations on including added sugars to labels. The term "added sugars" refer to sugars that are not naturally present in food. However, the regulations provide a loophole for manufacturers. It is ultimately left to the consumer on what to look for and how to spot added sugar ingredients. One problem is that added sugars are not included in the section for "Sugars" in the nutrient label. It is only listed in the ingredient's list at the bottom of the food label. It isn't required for manufacturers to place exactly how much added sugars were in the food. It is almost impossible for consumers to even guess the percentage of calories that are derived from these added sugars.

These loopholes also gave manufacturers chances to "hide" their added sugars. They use synonyms of added sugars, using about 3 to 4 different names. This way, they can place the sugar names at the end of the ingredient's list, since FDA guidelines only require to list ingredients according to percentage and not on how many calories they bring. For instance, even if fructose brings 78% of calories in just 0.5 mg, it will be listed further down the list based on the weight. Manufacturers can further place sugars down the list by using several synonyms to fructose, thereby further reducing the weight of each entry. An example is when making the ingredient's list of a packaged cookie. The added sugars total to 15 grams. This should be written at the head of the list. But to be able place it lower on the list, the manufacturer will break it down to 5 grams, malt syrup, 5 grams glucose and 5 grams invert sugar. This is dividing the sugar entry to mask it. Unsuspecting consumers would think that the product contains less sugar than what is actually in there. It is then up to the consumer to be able to hunt down these sugars and make a rough estimate of much sugar there really is.

Discerning Sugar Synonyms on Food Labels and Avoiding Them

Hunting down how much sugar is present in foods may prove to be a daunting task. It's near impossible to make an exact estimate. However, by knowing what terms refer to sugar, you can get general idea of how much there might be and not to be tricked by packaging and labeling strategies.

One of the easiest ways to spot a term that refers to sugar is one that needs in -*ose*. For exampl there is maltose, fructose, galactose, glucose solids, high fructose corn syrup, sucrose, dextrose ar lactose.

There are also some synonyms used for sugar without ending in the suffix -*ose*. Examples are th following:

- corn syrup
- cane juice
- cane juice crystals
- cane juice solids
- dehydrated cane juice
- dextrin
- dextran
- maltodextrin
- malt syrup
- refiner's syrup
- maple syrup
- carob syrup
- corn syrup solids
- beet sugar
- dehydrated fruit juice

- fruit juice concentrate

- fruit juice

- buttered syrup

- caramel

- brown sugar

- ethyl maltol

- yellow sugar

- date sugar

- barley malt

- turbinado

- golden syrup

- sorghum syrup

Healthy Alternatives

Like all other types of food, not all forms or type of sugar is bad. Some are healthy and can even help in restoring the normal, balanced state in the body. However, remember that not just because it's safe and healthy, the use is unlimited. Take in moderation to keep within the healthy effects.

Stevia

This is a natural, healthy sweetener that has been used for centuries in South America. It is also widely used in Japan, accounting for 41% of its sweetener market. Before "diet" versions of Coke were standardized by the Coca Cola Company, stevia was used as a healthy sugar substitute in Japan's version of Diet Coke. The source of the natural healthy sweetener is an herb, which grows native in South America.

Stevia recently got into trouble with the US FDA because of the label "sweetener". The issue has already been cleared and stevia is now among the top most popular alternative to sugar. Stevia is now classified as a dietary supplement in the US. This healthier sugar alternative has no calories. It also has no glycemic impact, which makes it suitable to use among diabetics. These characteristics are also perfect for those who are watching their weight and the eco-warriors.

Coconut Palm Sugar

Coconut palm sugar is produced by heating the sap of coconut palm. This process evaporates all the water content and the remaining granules become the coconut palm sugar. This is a nutritious natural alternative to white sugar. It has low glycemic index score, which means it does not rapidly spike glucose levels in the blood. This also means no buzz (sugar high) then a sudden crash (hypoglycemia or sudden drop in glucose levels in the blood).

The taste of coconut palm sugar is similar to brown sugar, but a little bit richer. This can be used in ways that brown sugar or white sugar is used.

Raw Honey

This has been part of many traditional healing practices. Raw honey has been used as treatment for various ailments like ulcers, seasonal allergies, and various digestion problems. Studies on raw honey found that it is rich in compounds that have antibiotic, antimicrobial and antibacterial properties. It also has astringent and anti-inflammatory characteristics. Aside from these, raw honey is also rich in nutrients such as minerals, amino acids, carbohydrates (the good kind), enzymes, antioxidants, phytonutrients and vitamins. Raw and unprocessed honey is already considered as one of nature's superfood. Not only is it a healthy, natural sweetener, it is also very beneficial for achieving overall health.

Molasses

Molasses is considered as "waste" by-product of making the traditional table sugar. It is that black, unattractive, highly concentrated syrup leftover from heating liquids like cane juice. The white crystals are taken and further processed into the table sugar everyone is familiar with. This one contains purely sugar and no nutrients. The dark molasses contains all the other nutrients such as fiber, minerals and vitamins. It is a rich source of calcium and iron. Molasses is thick and dark. It is most often used as a sweetener in place of sugar in a lot of baked goodies. Molasses is sweeter than table sugar so use less.

Artichoke Syrup

This natural sweetener is healthy and all-natural, with a special sweet taste. It contains a good amount of the nutrient inulin. This is one of the various types of fiber that supports healthy intestinal flora in the gut. This makes a great sweetener especially for people who are watching out for candida related issues and for those who need to be on a diabetic blood sugar monitoring. Studies have shown that inulin in artichoke syrup shows potential in improving calcium absorption in the gut. It can also help in improving the overall health of the gastrointestinal tract.

Lucuma powder

This is natural sweeteners that has a unique sweetness, fragrant and has a subtle taste that resembles maple syrup. It brings more life to dessert while keeping it healthy. It does not cause blood sugar levels to spike. Lucuma powder is a great source of healthy carbohydrates, minerals, fiber and vitamins. It also has large amounts of beta-carotene, making this natural sweetener a powerful immunity booster. Aside from this, lucuma is also high in vitamins B1 and B2, as well as iron. This sweetener has a low glycemic index. This makes it perfect for those with issues with their blood sugar levels such as those suffering from diabetes.

HINT

Even if these are natural and healthy, use in moderation. Anything in excess is always a bad idea. Healthy alternatives do not mean use is unlimited. Sweetening agents can overload the liver. Excess amounts can still get converted into fats.

Dealing with Sugar Cravings

Why is it easy for a person to develop a craving for sweets? Scientists say that it's hardwired into the system.

What Cause Sugar Cravings?

The taste perception for sweets is the very first one to develop in humans. It's because sweets are associated with carbohydrates, a nutrient essential during the early periods of life. Carbohydrates are sources of energy essential for normal body functions. Hence, the body does call for carbohydrates and sweets because of the energy it provides. Another reason for the development of cravings is that carbohydrates, particularly sweets stimulate the brain's reward center. It stimulates the release of serotonin, a brain neurotransmitter that is associated with good, positive feelings. Carbohydrates also stimulate the release of another feel-good compound in the brain called endorphins. These stimulate the rewards mechanism or system in the brain. These create a natural high, which gives the body a feeling of satisfaction and overall positive feeling. And by doing these, the brain and the body both seek to experience the positive effects over again- hence, the craving for sweets.

Carbohydrates cause all these, but not all carbs are the same. Some create intense cravings while some not quite so. For instance, carbohydrates from vegetables and whole grains provide the needed energy and promote satiety (feeling full and satisfied with a meal) sugars from some fruits and processed foods do not provide nutrients or energy, but stimulate the feel-good brain areas more intensely. Hence, these unhealthy sugars promote more intense cravings while providing nothing else to the body in terms of nutrition.

The main problem is not on the type of carbohydrate. It starts with the amount and frequency of sugar consumption. More sugar means a greater"high". The body has a tendency to prolong or repeat the process that produced the positive feeling. Most people consume an average of 22 teaspoons of added sugars per day. That means sugar that isn't naturally occurring in the foods they eat. The recommendation is to limit daily sugar intake to not more than 6 teaspoons for women and 9 teaspoons for men. The problem is, limiting sugar can be very difficult for a lot of people.

Limit Sugar Intake

Limiting sugar intake is very important in order to detoxify the body and to reset the body's normal balance. However, this may be difficult. Sugar is a highly addictive substance and getting "unhooked" requires help. It is a process that includes short-term steps and long-term practices. It also requires adequate knowledge about sugar, its effects and its sources, especially the hidden ones. A person has to be determined and fully dedicated to getting rid of sugar addiction.

Short-term techniques

Here are some immediate things that you can do in order to start your way towards recovering from sugar addiction and get rid of those sugar cravings:

- Give in, but just a little

Like most other addictions, going cold turkey isn't always the best way to go. One would have to deal intense cravings and at times, withdrawal symptoms. A person who has been consuming large amounts of sugar for a long time may find the cravings getting so intense. Concentration is difficult because the person is preoccupied with the cravings. Energy levels fall because the body is not used to using alternative sources of energy like fats. Discomforts like fatigue, inability to focus, overwhelming desire to eat and other similar discomforts may become so intense that the person can no longer perform daily tasks comfortably. For this, it is better to gradually decrease sugar intake instead of sudden, "cold turkey" style.

Give in a little to the craving. Eat a small cookie or a fun-sized chocolate or candy bar. Enjoy in small amounts to avoid feeling deprived. Feelings of deprivation make the journey even more frustrating, difficult and less successful. Also, be mindful and make sure not to go overboard. Sometimes, people may find themselves slipping into old habits and reaching for more sugary foods. Take little nibbles of the sugary treat. The body will be able to have ample time to process and savor the sweet treat. After a small piece of treat, pause for a while. Drink a glass of water. If the craving still persists, engage in activities that take the mind off the craving.

- Learn to combine different foods

At times, giving up on sweets like candy bars, cookies and all those delectable sweet snacks and desserts can be an overwhelming thought. Nutrition experts recommend mixing sweets and health foods when satisfying cravings. For example, dip a fresh banana in melted dark chocolate to satisf cravings. Again, take in moderation. Just because bananas and dark chocolates can bring healt benefits, it does not mean it's ok to gorge on it. Another example is baking your own cookies instea of buying. When baking, add healthy almonds and use healthier sugar instead of white refined sugar.

- Going cold-turkey

Some people are successful in cutting out sugar and stopping sugar cravings by going cold turke If opting to use this method, expect that the toughest period will be the first 48 to 72 hours after th last sugar intake. The longer you go on a no-sugar diet, the easier it will be. Sheer determination key.

- Eating gum

Chewing some gum can help in reducing cravings, according to some research. But this techniqu is not highly recommended because chewing gum has been found linked to the development dental problems like tooth decay.

- Eat fruits

Fruits are naturally sweet. It's nature's dessert entree. The natural sugar effectively satisfi cravings. Along with the natural sugars, fiber, vitamins, minerals, and with the right choic antioxidants and phytonutrients can be obtained as well. It would be great to prepare thes beforehand and carry them round so that when the cravings hit, they're immediately accessible. Ha slices of fruits like apples and pears, or a few pieces of bananas, a mixture of berries, etc. also, ha some died fruits like raisins, and a handful of seeds and/or nuts.

- Walk

As was mentioned previously, if the cravings hit, get up and walk away. Talk a walk around th room, hallway, or if, possible, outdoors around the block or nearby park. The mind becomes focus on something else other than the craving.

- Making the right choice: quality over quantity

When cravings hit, satisfy them with a carefully chosen sugary treat. For example, when satisfyi a craving, reach for a small nugget of dark chocolate (at least 70% cocoa content, which is healthy) instead of a large-sized candy bar. Eat slowly and savor the taste instead of popping it all in the mouth and chewing it fast.

- Eating regularly

Eat at regular hours. If the interval between main meals is too long, the body will interpret it as a threat to its energy stores. It will signal for a need to eat sugary foods because sugary foods can provide quick energy, which the body thinks it needs for a perceived energy crisis. Also, regular eating assures the body there is an incoming supply of energy so there is no need to signal for quick sugary foods.

Try to eat every 3-5 hours. This helps to stabilize the levels of sugar in the blood. Irrational eating behaviors will also be perceived as a threat that can lead to an energy crisis, which will prompt the body to seek sugary foods. Eat healthy foods and stock on proteins and fibers like those found in fresh produce and whole grains.

Notice that these techniques promote eating. However, it is very different from overeating. These techniques promote making the right, healthy choices to food and to eat at regular times. It also promotes breaking up meals, hence, the 3-5-hour eating schedule. For example, eat breakfast with quinoa (whole grain) and some nuts. The yogurt or breakfast smoothie can be saved later, as a mid-morning energy-boosting snack. For lunch, eat proteins and vegetable salads, saving dessert for a mid-afternoon snack.

Long Term Techniques for Curbing Cravings

Long-term techniques help to stay off sugar-laden foods for the rest of your life. The following techniques can help to sustain a living a craving-free, sugar-free lifestyle.

- Avoid artificial sweeteners

Artificial sweeteners may be considered by most as healthy alternatives. However, remember that anything artificial is never good for health. Studies have found that these artificial sweeteners do not necessarily lessen the cravings. These also have been demonstrated to be linked to the development of obesity.

- Rewarding yourself

One of the greatest reasons for developing a liking to sugars is its ability to stimulate the brain's reward system. Make the process of curing sugar addiction more rewarding and positive so that the brain will not fight the idea of going sugar-free. Reward the self for every milestone and after achieving specific personal goals. The reward may either be big or small. It's a great way to make the brain associate the process of fighting cravings a rewarding, positive experience.

- Slow down and plan

A carefully planned method for curbing cravings is more successful than diving headlong into the process without a clear idea of the entire process. Diet mayhem results from a poorly constructed diet plans. Slow down and take careful assessment of your current diet. Check what needs to be removed, changed or retained. Also, planned meals are more successful in achieving health and weight goals. It also helps in preventing emotional eating- eating when angry frustrated, stressed or depressed.

- Support

A good support system increases the chances of being successful in achieving health and weight goals. Having someone to talk to can help to prevent emotional eating, because the mind and body is more preoccupied in verbalizing and venting out emotions. It's easier to limit mouthfuls of ice cream when talking to a friend about emotional issues.

- Mixing things up

No single technique can give all goals. When one technique does not seem to work, try another. It takes trail-and-error to find the technique that works best for you. Each person has unique responses and one method may not necessarily work in the same way in others.

HINT: *Remember why you are doing this. If you are tempted to take a bite of that cake, hit the snooze button or cancel your gym appointment, take a minute to remember your goals (which should be posted on your refrigerator) Before you act, ask yourself "Is this going to help or hurt me?" It won't always be easy and there will be some really tough days but just remember, YOU are in control, and if the answer to your question is that this will hurt you, then take a minute and then make the right decision for you that will enable you to reach your wedding day goals.*

Cutting out Flour

Aside from sugar, flour is also a health concern. Flour is considered as the second "sugar" because it has the same negative effect in the body. Foods made with flour or used flour is not sweet, but the effects are the same. Flour gets converted into sugar by the body and the cycle continues. More flour means more sugar is produced. This leads to spikes in blood glucose levels. It's essentially the same pathway as sugar.

Understanding White or Refined Flour

White or refined flour is produced from wheat. The grains undergo various manufacturing process in order to produce the white powdered stuff. The flour is essentially stripped off of all fiber and nutrients. It does not spoil or go rancid because there is nothing in it that can spoil because everything is essentially lifeless. It is used as a binding agent that holds artificial colors, preservatives, flavors, additives, sodium, sugar and other ingredients together. White flour is fat-free and low in calories. People think food made from it is also healthy. It's not. Flour is low in fat, cholesterol and calories because it does not contain anything at all, it's empty of everything. But even if white flour is empty and lifeless, food made from flour can actually lead to poor health.

Negative Effects in the Body

Flour is like white sugar because it is closely linked to the development of various health problems. Frequent and large consumption can also increase the risk factors for health problems such as obesity and diabetes.

Nutritional deficiency

People who frequently eat foods that contain white flour are at higher risk for nutrient deficiencies. This is a huge irony considering that whole wheat is very nutritious. The process whole wheat grains go through to be converted into flour strips off a lot of nutrients such as fiber, potassium, B vitamins, zinc, calcium, vitamin E, manganese and copper. Some manufacturers attempt to bring back some nutrients to refined flour by fortifying it or enriching. Yet, the fortification or enriching process uses synthetic chemicals, which is not at all similar to natural nutrients. For instance, a popular processed, instant spaghetti brand boasts of supplying 8essential nutrients. In an attempt to restore lost nutrients during the processing and to "improve" the nutritional value of junk food, it adds synthetic nutrients. One particular added nutrient is synthetic B vitamins. These are derived from coal tar. These synthetic vitamins may cause imbalances in the body rather than nourish it. A person consumes this processed, instant, ready-to-eat spaghetti, thinking it already provides the body's daily needs for B vitamins. This idea leads to false sense of assurance that the body is already getting the vitamins it needs. This can lead to imbalances in vitamin B, manifested by poor memory, muscle tenderness, depression, fatigue, irritability, anxiety, insomnia and heart palpitations.

Blood Sugar Problems

Eating too much of the unhealthy type of sugar can lead to imbalance in blood sugar and to the development of hormonal problems. White flour is quickly converted into sugar, which stimulates the same process as white sugar. Hence, eating a lot of flour-based food can also lead to problems when it comes to regulating the levels of sugar in the blood.

Often, flour is even more dangerous than sugar. It's easier for people to stay away from sugar just by staying from sweet foods. Flour is more difficult because it is found in so many foods. It isn't just present in sweet foods. It is also used in savory foods. It's not just present in snacks and desserts. It can also be present in the simple dips and dressing used with healthier foods like salads. It's practically everywhere and it can be difficult to identify foods that contain flour.

For instance, a lot of people are actively staying away from sugary foods. But they still don't get the results they want such as lower blood sugar levels and weight loss. The answer might be because diet is rich in refined flour. Some even try to defend their meals consisting of pasta, bagels, pizza, and even the croutons on their vegetable salads. Sure, there isn't anything sweet in it but the flour in these foods gets converted into sugar. The body has no capability of differentiating sugar from white sugar to sugar made from flour. What it does recognize is that both foods create spikes in blood sugar levels. Hence, the body will have the same reactions. Eating a plate of pasta will still cause sugar crash in the same way as a slice of moist chocolate cake.

Constipation

Get a cup of white flour and add 4 tablespoons of water. You get a thick paste. That's a rough estimate of what happens to all the white flour in the foods you ate. This paste moves slowly through the digestive tract, which promotes constipation.

Another thing about white flour that promotes constipation is its lack of fiber. Fiber draws water towards itself, forming bulk and makes the passage of stool easy and fast. Without fiber, flour in the digestive tract cannot absorb sufficient amounts of water to help it move faster.

When a person is constipated, waste is retained longer in the body. Consider this: a person having bowel movement once every other day means at least a day's worth of waste is always inside the body. The body is also designed to remove waste as often as it is formed. Theoretically, if a person eats 3 main meals a day, bowel movements is also 3 times. It is a very simple idea. However, due to lifestyle and diet, this isn't always the case. Ideally, there should be at least one bowel movement each day. This would mean that waste accumulated for the day is flushed out. Longer than this would mean that the body is storing a lot of waste. This would then find its way to the blood and eventually the tissues. There, this reabsorbed waste would cause increased fat conversion and storage. It also increases the risk for health problems like obesity, cancer and other serious illnesses.

Replacing White Flour

Just as with white sugar, white or refined flour should be limited, if not entirely avoided. The following are simple steps that can help you do that:

Limiting flour-based products to not more than 3 times a week

White flour is present in almost every commercial, processed food item. Learn to read labels and stay away from items that contain refined flour. By limiting consumption, the negative effects can be limited as well. This is just the first step to ultimately getting rid of flour from the diet.

Replace white pasta or bread with whole grain varieties

Avoid things made with enriched flour. Do not be fooled by the label "enriched" or "fortified" because the added "nutrients" are artificial and will do more harm to the body than good. Instead of buying white bread or white pasta, buy those made with whole grain. However be mindful still because most of the commercial whole grain food varieties contain other unhealthy ingredients such as hydrogenated oils and HFCS or high fructose corn syrup.

Choose food made with whole kernel grains

This is more preferred than buying whole grains already made into flour. Again, the process may also strip away the fiber and other nutrients from the grains. Choose those made with unbroken grains like quinoa, hulled barley, whole wheat berries, millet, wild rice and buckwheat groats. These have more complex structures compare to processed grains, which means they do not get quickly converted into simple sugars in the body. The slower digestion of these whole grains means they do not cause a rapid spike in blood sugar levels and won't cause sugar crash. The complexity of these structures also enables them to retain as much nutrients such as fiber, minerals and vitamins. Hence they are much more nutritious than their processed counterparts. In addition to the nutrients, eating whole grains help in feeling full early into the meal. This helps to limit how much food I eaten. For example, a person would usually feel full after eating 3 to 4slices of white bread, hunger strikes usually within an hour after eating. So, there is a tendency to overeat or to eat more frequently. These foods gets quickly converted into sugar and eventually stored in fatty tissues. This adds more weight. On the other hand, whole grains help with portion control. People would already feel full with just a slice or two. Hunger strikes again longer compared to when eating white bread. It may take more than an hour before hunger strikes. Also, when eating white bread for breakfast, for example, mid-morning slump is often experienced. There is poor focus and energy, along with a craving for sweet food. When eating whole grains for breakfast, mid-morning slump is unlikely to occur.

Try to add sprouted grains

Sprouted grains contain enzymes that can be beneficial to the body. The spouting process activates these chemicals from within the grains. During this period, enzymes act on the starch within the grains and convert it into maltose. When eaten, the body has an easier time in digesting it. More nutrients from the sprouted grains are also absorbed by the body because these are already pre-digested. Also, sprouted grains have more protein contents that are easily absorbed and used by the body.

Replace white flour with seed or nut meals

These make perfect substitutes to white flour for baking. Examples include ground almonds, flax, coconut and cashews. Aside from baking, nut and/or seed meals also make healthier substitutes for breading on seafood or meats.

Use whole grain flours

Stick to using real whole grain fours. These flours should still have all the contents of a whole grain, such as the germ, the bran and the endosperm. Usually, real whole grain flours are coarse and have some discolorations. They are not snow white in color and not very fine powder. However, these are still processed but are much healthier than refined flours. Whole grain flours also have almost the same glycemic index are white flour because the components are already broken down into fine materials, making them easier to digest and absorb. Consequently, these can cause rapid rise in blood sugar levels. This is the only downside of using whole grain flours. They are, however, much healthier and more nutritious than white flour. To get different kinds of nutrients, choose mixed whole grain flours, such as a mix of buckwheat, oats and barley.

Go flour-free

White flour is present in processed commercial foods. Go flour-free by opting to buy whole, real, unprocessed foods. Notice an improvement in health, as well as a step towards better weight management. Instead of eating flour-based breakfast meals, go for whole food like fruits or eggs.

Instead of eating a sandwich, ditch the bread. Eat vegetable salads instead of wraps.

(Optional) Performing a Colon Cleanse

NOTE: If you decide to do either of the following cleanses, it is better to do this at the very beginning of your weight loss journey. This will better prepare your body and will aid in the weight loss process

What actually happens in the colon if stool is not regularly and properly flushed out? It remains in the colon. While in the colon, water and a few other compounds are reabsorbed into the blood. The longer stool stays in the colon, the more wastes enter the blood and get deposited into the tissues.

Colon cleansing is a very old health practice. It has been around since the time of Ancient Greece. The practice has continued until modern times. In the 1920s and 1930s, colon cleansing became popular in the US. In the next decades, the popularity has waned as theories supporting this practice lost the support of the scientific community. Recent years saw resurgence in colon cleansing because research findings have demonstrated the benefits.

Goal of Natural Colon Cleansing

Colon cleansing is ultimately to remove toxins and waste that remain stagnant in the colon. If allowed to stay in the gut, these accumulated wastes and toxins can cause a lot of problems. It can interfere with normal body processes and increase the risk for several illnesses. And by removing these stagnant wastes, the following benefits can be achieved:

- improved vitality
- improved mental or cognitive functioning
- improved immunity
- weight loss
- reduced risk for cancers like cancer of the colon
- improved digestion
- removal of toxins

46

Steps in Natural Colon-Cleansing

To start a colon cleanse, stop eating solid foods. Rest the bowel so that it can put most of its energies in eliminating wastes that have accumulated within the entire tract. Liquids will be the main source of nourishment. Nutrients in liquid form are easier to digest and absorb. It also has very little waste (undigested materials) that can add to the wastes that the colon or gut is trying to get rid of.

On this day, taking a cleansing juice or smoothie helps to further expel anything that got stuck to the bowels. An example is this recipe:

Apple, Psyllium and Ginger Colon-Cleansing Juice

Ingredients:

- Apples

- 1 teaspoon of ground ginger

- 1 teaspoon of ground psyllium husk

Procedure:

- Juice apples, enough to obtain about 8 ounces of apple juice

- Add the ground ginger and ground psyllium husk to apple juice.

- Mix thoroughly until well blended. Psyllium husk may cause some gel-like formation. Keep mixing until the consistency is smooth and even. It might be easier if blending this cleansing juice in a blender.

In this recipe, psyllium binds with the toxins in the gut and brings then out for excretion. Ginger helps in flushing out any stagnant or stuck toxins within the colon. Apple is rich in fiber that stimulates peristalsis and expulsion of wastes from the colon.

Day 12: Slowly reintroduce regular foods. Start with easy to digest foods, such as simple smoothies. Avoid eating too much fiber because this can cause bloating, diarrhea and cramps. Also, avoid fats and tough proteins to prevent cramps, gas, bloating, nausea, vomiting and other gastric discomforts.

All throughout the colon-cleanse, keep hydrated. The body needs water in order to efficiently flush out the toxins and to prevent dehydration.

(Optional) Perform a Liver Cleanse

A liver is cleanse is promoting the more efficient function of this organ to detoxify the body. This is often done along with a colon cleanse because the activities and guidelines are pretty much the same. The difference lies in what herbs or foods were taken during the cleanse. Herbs taken are those that support liver health and in promoting detoxification.

Start in the same way as colon cleanse. Stop eating unhealthy foods and rest the bowel.

Drink a liver cleansing smoothie or juice, such as the following recipe:

Lemon Liver Cleansing Juice

Ingredients:

- ½ teaspoon of cayenne pepper
- 4 tablespoons of lemon juice, freshly squeezed
- ½ teaspoon of organic maple syrup

Procedure:

- Place cayenne in a 10-ounce glass
- Add lemon juice.
- Fill the drinking glass with warm water.
- Stir the juice mixture thoroughly.
- Add maple syrup and mix until well combined.

Drink this cleansing juice on an empty stomach for optimum results. Cayenne stimulates the body's metabolism while supporting the emptying of the colon. This promotes the fast expulsion of any toxins from the body via the stool. Lemon juice stimulates the liver to remove more toxins from the blood. Maple syrup has anti-inflammatory effects to reduce any inflammation triggered by the mobilization of the toxins from the tissues.

Eating Whole Organic Foods and Superfoods

Organic foods are those raised without using artificial chemicals. This includes agricultural products that were raised without the application of synthetic pesticides or fertilizers. These synthetic chemicals leave residue on the leaves, flowers, stems or fruits. When eaten, these residues are toxins in the body. It increases the risk for serious illnesses like cancer. It also creates imbalance in the hormones, which also promotes more fat production and accumulation.

Eating Organic Foods

Stay away from foods that are not certified organic, especially if eating the fresh produce with the peel still on. The safest way to go is to buy foods that are whole and does not come in a package. Also, if possible, ask where the fresh produce comes from. Then check out the far itself or go online to see any reviews about the place.

Superfoods to Start Adding to Meals

Superfoods are nutritionally-packed natural foods that promote healing and protection. These are foods that also contain antioxidants that fight off infections, enhance the removal of toxins and protect the tissues from free radical-damage. Vegetables and fruits that have bright colors are most often the ones that have the highest concentrations of antioxidants. Examples include:

- raspberries

- blueberries

- kale

- tomatoes

- spinach

- carrots

- eggplant

- butternut squash

- oranges

- apples

- sweet potatoes

Some of these superfoods also have omega-3 fatty acids that promote decreases inflammatio protect the heart and improve overall health. Examples include:

- tuna

- salmon

- almonds

- avocado

- flax seeds

- walnuts

- olive oil

Eating the Right Fats

Fats are not always unhealthy. It is one of the macronutrients that the body needs. In the body, fats are used in making important hormones. It is also needed for cellular processes, like being part of cellular maintenance (particularly the cell membrane, which is actually mostly fat molecules), cell signaling system and nerve structure maintenance.

Healthy Fats

Here are the top 5 fats to use to achieve a healthier body. These can also help in losing weight by helping with portion control and prolonging the period before hunger sets in.

Coconut Oil

Coconut oil is rich in nutrients and compounds that promote health and weight loss. This has a variety of uses, such as healthy oil for baking and general cooking. It can also be added to healthy foods like oatmeal and smoothies.

Compounds in coconut oil offer anti-cancer, anti-microbial and antibacterial benefit in the body. The oils actually help reduce inflammation in the body. The active compounds also improve nutrient absorption, intestinal health and digestion. Coconut oil also demonstrated ability in lowering the risk for type 2 diabetes and cardiovascular diseases. It also helps in promoting better health of the liver and the kidneys. Coconut oil also has supportive effects on the immune system. It also helps in better weight management, improving energy and in revving up the metabolic rate.

A lot of people are hesitant about using coconut oil once they find out about the saturated fats in it. Saturated fats have been cast in a bad light because they cause all sorts of problems like high cholesterol levels, high blood pressure, and related cardiovascular problems. It is also linked to the development of cancers and obesity.

Coconut oil does have significant amount of saturated fats. But these saturated fats behave differently from those found in animal products. They do not cause the same negative effects. The triglycerides in coconut oil are medium-chain. This type is easily metabolized by the body. Furthermore, medium-chain triglycerides can be used by the body as a source of energy, reducing the chances of it getting converted into fatty deposits in the tissues. This type of fatty acids also shows that it can help in boosting the metabolic rate resulting in better fat metabolism, weight management, increase in the levels of good cholesterol called HDL (high density lipoprotein) and in protecting against risk factors of cardiovascular diseases.

Nut Oils

Nuts are great for health. It is a go-to quick healthy snack. It is rich in healthy carbohydrates, proteins and fats, as well as minerals and vitamins. It is very diet-friendly, no matter what type of weight loss diet is followed.

One particular healthy fat in nuts is alpha linolenic acid. This is one type of omega-3 fatty acid, a heart-healthy fat compound.

Nuts are also great sources for the amino acid L-arginine. This compound boosts immunity, improves the function of the blood vessels, and promotes faster wound healing. It also contributes to the management of cardiovascular illnesses.

Aside from healthy fats and proteins, nuts also have vitamin E and soluble fiber. This type of fiber readily dissolves in water and helps in easing passage of stool through the digestive tract. Soluble fibers also have cholesterol-lowering effects. It also helps in regulating the levels of glucose in the body. Vitamin E acts as a powerful antioxidant that brings several health benefits. It promotes normal proper functioning of the immune system. It also helps with DNA repair. Vitamin E is also known for its positive effects on the skin, promoting healthy, youthful and glowing skin.

Great nuts to include are Brazil nuts, walnuts and almonds. These can snacked on alone. They make perfect healthy protein sources for smoothies. These are also great to add to whole healthy meals like salads as healthy sources of fats, proteins and carbohydrates. They also add texture and flavor to make meals more interesting. Another way to enjoy nuts is through eating nut butters. These make great dips to enliven vegetable snacks like carrot and celery sticks.

Avocados

These are nutritionally packed fruits that contain healthy types of fats. Before, avocados had been considered as unhealthy because of its high fat content. Further studies revealed that the type of fat found in avocados is of the healthy type. It has a number of health benefits, such as providing healthy fat molecules the body can use as energy or as part of its various cellular processes. The fats in avocados are also known for its inflammation-lowering effects that can help in reducing weight and reducing the risk for health problems like cancer, obesity, cardiovascular disorders, stroke and type 2 diabetes, amongst others.

Another beneficial compound in avocados is the antioxidant glutathione. In the body, glutathione helps in cleansing the body, detoxifying several kinds of toxins and altering them for easy excretion. This antioxidant is very effectual in removing heavy metals and free radicals from the tissues. Also, glutathione plays an important role in slowing the aging process and in maintaining the healthy function of the immune system.

Folate is another beneficial compound in avocados. It has been demonstrated in various studies as helpful in decreasing the incidence of stroke and heart diseases. It is also high in vitamin E.

Great ways to eat avocados is to eat as it is or make into delectable, nutritious guacamole. Slice them up and ad to fresh salads or to smoothies.

Seeds

Like nuts, seeds are also great sources of healthy fats. They are rich in omega-3 fatty acids that have positive protective effects on the cardiovascular system. These are also rich in fibers and proteins. These are also packed with minerals that promote health such as zinc, selenium and magnesium.

Examples of seeds to include in the diet are chia seeds, sunflower seeds, pumpkin and flax seeds. Chia seeds are actually among the superfoods, a group of foods known for their potent compounds that promote several health benefits in the body. It also has an excellent nutrition profile. It contains large amounts of healthy, heart-friendly omega-3 fatty acids. These are also high in fiber, antioxidants, zinc, iron, copper, manganese, phosphorus and magnesium.

There are so many ways to use seeds. These can be added to smoothies as added proteins and to give it more texture and flavor. These can be added to baked healthy goodies, salad bars and trail mixes. Seeds are also excellent to add in salads. Healthy cuts of meat can be crusted with seeds and baked for more interesting flavors and textures.

Olive Oil

This is very healthy oil that promotes numerous health benefits. It is high in monounsaturated fats that support the heart and has protective effects on the cardiovascular system. These are also high in antioxidants such as vitamin E, carotenoids and chlorophyll.

The fats in olive oil are healthy energy sources for the body. It can lower cholesterol levels, reducing the risk for cholesterol-related diseases. It helps in the management of diabetes and in cancer prevention. Olive oil also helps in reducing and managing inflammatory conditions like arthritis. People with asthma also find their symptoms decrease when using olive oil.

The best form of olive oil is extra virgin. This term means that the oil has undergone minimal processing. Extra virgin olive oil has retained as much of the original nutrients in its most natural form.

There are so many ways to use olive oil. This is very versatile and can be used for cooking, as a dressing or as part of dips. These can be used in baking and sautéing, too. For example, add a few teaspoons of olive oil and apple cider vinegar, along with a small amount of garlic, pepper and red onions. Mix this simple vinaigrette and pour over fresh salad greens. Use this as a healthy fat ingredient in homemade mayonnaise made with fresh organic eggs. Or, use in making fresh Hollandaise sauce and spoon over hard-boiled eggs.

Extra virgin olive oil has a distinct taste that can be overpowering. To add to the versatility of this healthy oil, adding herbs can change, mask or enhance the taste of olive oil. Slightly heat olive oil and pour it into a jar or container filled with herb of choice like rosemary, basil, garlic, oregano, or a mix of various herbs.

Eating the Right Carbs

Carbohydrates are also among the major macronutrients that the body needs in order to grow and develop normally as well as function properly. But like most other nutrients, not all carbohydrates are the same. Some have good effects on the body while some are just as bad as sugar and flour.

Bad Carbohydrates

Carbohydrates that are bad for health are those that are simple. These usually have high glycemic index scores. These simple carbohydrates are readily absorbed and converted by the body into sugar. Again, this will cause spikes in blood glucose levels and set off an unhealthy cycle of high sugar- high insulin-sugar crash-hunger-and so on.

Bad carbohydrates include sweets, foods with added sugars, processed foods, and those made with refined flour.

Good Carbohydrates

The complex carbohydrates are the best ones to add to daily meals. These are slowly digested by the body. This type of carbohydrate does not create sugar spikes and sugar crash. These also provide a steady supply of energy to the body, eliminating the need to eat too frequently. Complex carbohydrates help a person to feel full longer after a meal. This way, a person can be more successful in losing weight through portion control. Best carbs are those from whole grains, legumes and vegetables.

Eating the Right Proteins

Proteins, like fats and carbohydrates, are also important macronutrients. The body needs it fo several crucial processes such as hormone synthesis and regulation, growth and development o tissues, repair of organs and in cellular transport and signaling. Not all proteins are bad and no everything is bad for health.

The problem is not about the type of protein but more on the source of protein. Most anim proteins also come with a high amount of unhealthy saturated fats. Also, animal sources may hav been raised with loads of antibiotics and synthetic hormones. Antibiotics are often given to prote livestock and poultry from common infections that often wipe out entire farms. Synthetic hormon are often given to improve meat quality, such as improving the meat to fat ratio (more lean meat ar less fat), promote more milk production and to bulk up the animals. These drugs and hormon become part of the meat and the animal products (such as milk and milk-based food products, egg etc.). When eaten, they create imbalance and cause fat accumulation, excess weight gain ar difficulty with losing weight. These also increase the risk for cancers, stroke and other relate illnesses.

Best Protein Sources

The best protein sources are those from omega-3 rich sources like the following:

- salmon
- trout
- mackerel
- tuna
- sardines
- herring

Other good sources are plant proteins. These are present in good amounts in beans, nuts a seeds.

Eggs are excellent protein sources. It has all the 20 essential amino acids, with the good types fat in it to help improve the absorption of these amino acids. Choose eggs that came from grass-fed, free range chicken.

For animal protein sources, choose those from organically raised, grass-fed, free range animals. The white meat part of poultry, like chicken and turkey. For beef and pork, choose the parts that have less fat in them.

Eating Healing Herbs

Herbs can help the body in healing itself. Even people who are not currently suffering from any illness will benefit. Most often, a lot of people are unaware that they have inflammatory conditions or some other problem in their bodies. These illnesses are often masked by weight gain and discomforts that are easily regarded as common and related to daily activities. For example, people with frequent headaches think that this is only due to their activities and not because they have health problems. People with digestive problems often attribute their discomforts to something they ate. For most of these, the accumulation of toxins is the root cause. People who gain a lot of weight and those who find it hard to lose excess weight are also often unaware that all those stubborn fats are due to some injury or inflammation in the body. To improve health and speedup weight loss, allow and support the body to heal itself. Herbs are perfect for this job.

The following herbs have long been known for their healing properties and should be incorporated into daily meals. By healing the body, it can already start to shed off the protective layers of fat and start losing excess weight.

- Turmeric: Best made into tea and drank 2 to 3 times per day. Bioactive compounds speed up metabolism and promote weight loss. Turmeric also has anti-cancer, anti-viral, antibacterial, antibiotic and anti-inflammatory effects that promote healing.

- Dandelion: Often also made into tea. Compounds help to reduce inflammation and boost immune function.

- Garlic: Promotes healing with its potent anti-viral and antibiotic properties. Garlic can be added to food, cooked or raw. Some people can eat raw garlic alone for increased and immediate effects.

- Cilantro: A popular Asian herb that has anti-inflammatory and healing properties in the body. This can be added to salads or to smoothies.

- Basil: A popular leafy herb that promote reduction in inflammation in the body. This is a key ingredient in pesto sauce, mixed with healthy olive oil and used as dips or dressings.

- Milk thistle: This is a popular herb made into tea that helps in promoting better digestion. It is also helpful in reliving gastrointestinal discomforts such bloating and cramps, as well as constipation.

- Chamomile: This is among the most popular and widely used herb for relieving gastrointestinal problems. Made into tea, chamomile helps to relieve gas, bloating and indigestion. By promoting healing of the gut, the body is better able to digest, absorb and metabolize food.

Rev Up Your Metabolism with Food

Metabolism is affected by the type of food you eat. Sluggish metabolism means your body is more about stacking up on fats and refusing to burn its stores for energy. To speed up weight loss, you have to rev up your metabolic rates.

Foods That Improve Metabolism

Most other weight loss diets only focus on eliminating unhealthy carbohydrates, refined sugar, white flour, processed foods and unhealthy fats. These can promote substantial fat loss. Revving up metabolism will further increase weight loss and keep fat off. There a lot of foods that can be added into the diet. These are everyday simple foods that can bring excellent results in less time than when not using them at all. Foods that help in increasing the body's metabolic rates include the following:

Lemon Juice

This is a very effective food that works wonder with metabolism. It helps promote better digestive process, which makes it a popular morning beverage in Japan. They mix hot water and lemon, making into a tea. Lemon helps to detoxify the body while improving the metabolic rate, promoting greater weight loss.

Another way to use lemon to rev up metabolism is by taking a few tablespoons of freshly squeezed lemon juice right before a meal. It promotes stomach acidity, which helps food to be digested faster. It also lowers the body's response to sugar produced from a meal, reducing the cycle that promotes sugar spikes and fat accumulation. This same effect is also observed when taking lemon juice during a meal. Another way to use lemon juice is to add a few tablespoons of fresh lemon juice to a glass of sparkling water. Drink during a meal. Another very simple way is to squeeze fresh lemon over salads or meats and fishes. The acidity helps to break down nutrients, making them more readily absorbed by the body.

Cinnamon

This is a delicious spice that has profound effects in the body. It has antibacterial, antimicrobial and anti-inflammatory effects. Aside from these, cinnamon is also a very effective spice in improving the body's metabolic rates, promoting greater weight loss. Adding cinnamon to food also helps to curb sugar cravings. It also improves blood sugar balance and insulin sensitivity.

To use, sprinkle a teaspoon or two over breakfast cereals or egg dishes. Add them to herbal teas. Or, just mix a pinch of cinnamon powder to a teaspoon of raw honey and eat. Do this before or after a meal, or when sugar cravings hit.

Kefir

This is a cultured food that contains beneficial bacteria. Kefir and other fermented or cultured foods can help deal with sugar cravings. It also promotes better digestive health by enhancing the function and condition of the healthy bacterial population within the gut. Good digestive process improves metabolism. It also helps the body to use nutrients form food better, promoting better health and supports weight loss.

If the bacterial colony in the gut is not well-balanced, food is not properly broken down. More calories are extracted from food, especially the empty ones. Then these calories are quickly turned into fat. A healthy population of good bacteria in the gut helps the body to choose the better nutrients and then utilize them more efficiently instead of turning them into fat and storing them.

Be careful when buying kefir and other cultured food products. Some may have included sugars or other unhealthy ingredients. Also, the bacterial cultures may no longer be viable. For example, yogurt is a kind of cultured product that can increase metabolism. However, commercial yogurt may contain sugars and gluten as stabilizer, colorant or flavoring. Check where and how the product was made.

Cayenne pepper

Cayenne pepper revs up the metabolism, helping the body to burn more calories. The heat in cayenne pepper increases the body's rate of burning through calories. This helps to increase the rate of fat burning and weight loss. Eating cayenne pepper and other kinds of hot peppers helps to improve satiety in meals while helping with portion control. You eat less but you feel more satisfied with your meal. For the more adventurous, add a pinch (or more) of cayenne powder to smoothies. Mix raw chocolate powder with coconut milk and avocado. Add cayenne pepper for a good kick.

Coconut milk and coconut oil

These are kitchen staples for a person determined to follow a healthy lifestyle and diet. These can be used for everything from healthy fats in cooking to making shakes or smoothies. The milk and oil have antibacterial and anti-viral properties that protect the body from infections. It also has numerous nutrients that can help in increasing metabolism. It balances the gut bacterial population which play crucial roles in regulating metabolic activities in the body.

Smoothies

Smoothies are nutritionally packed. They can help cleanse, detoxify and improve the body's overall health. It is recommended to replace one main meal with a smoothie per day in order to achieve your health goals.

When incorporating smoothies into the daily diet plan, it is best to make time to make one yourself. Buying ready-made smoothies or pre-packed ones is putting yourself at risk for drinking synthetic chemicals. Most commercially prepared smoothies contain additives, colorants, preservatives and other similar compounds in order to prolong shelf life and improve taste. It's best to stay away from these.

Dedicate time to preparing smoothies. It is advisable to make smoothie in the morning. Taking one early in the day helps to prime the body for the day's activities. It will help to boosts energy levels and speeds up the metabolism to give the body the energy it needs for the day. This also leads to greater weight loss.

Green Smoothie Recipe

To get started on a smoothie diet, try this simple recipe:

Ingredients:

- 1 piece of medium-sized ripe banana

- 1 cup of kale or collard greens, tightly packed into the measuring cup, coarsely chopped

- ½ cup parsley leaves, lightly packed

- 1 piece of medium-sized Granny Smith apple, cored and coarsely chopped, leave the peel on (where most of the fiber contents are present)

- 2 ¼ cups of clean drinking water

Procedure:

- Place all ingredients in a blender.

- Pulse until everything has been incorporated smoothly and evenly.

- Add more water to adjust the thickness or viscosity of the smoothie.

- Drink immediately.

It is highly advisable to drink smoothies within a few hours. In fact, the best time to consume a smoothie is right after it is made. This way, the broken up nutrients will still be fresh and active. Waiting longer before drinking the prepared smoothies would open it to spoilage, bacterial contamination and inactivation of the nutrient contents.

For more Smoothie recipes see my book "Superfood Smoothies"

(Optional) Try the 5:2 Plan

Fasting is not about starvation or not eating anything. It just means limiting solid food and giving the digestive system a rest from all the rigors of digestion. The goal of fasting is to reset the body's natural homeostatic functions. This can also support weight loss goals further.

One of the most popular fasting methods is intermittent fasting or the 5:2 plan. In this plan, a person eats normally for 5 days a week and fasts for 2 days. The 2-day fasting period may be 2 consecutive days or 2 separate days of the week. One can opt to fast for 2 consecutive days during the weekends. Some may find it easier to fast for 2 separate days, such as fast on a Tuesday and then on Saturday.

Guidelines to Fasting

The fast can be as long as 48 hours or as short as 8 hours. It depends on individual goals and tolerance. Beginners are recommended to fast for 8 to 12 hours before attempting to fast longer. Start with the last meal of the previous day. Some people find it easier to start the fast after dinner. For example, they eat dinner at 8PM, counting the hours start from this last meal. They sleep for most of the fasting period, which is a very natural thing to do. So if they go to sleep at 10PM, they start counting their fasting hour. When they wake up the next day at 6am, they have already completed an 8-hour fast, sweat-free and no hassle or much difficulty. Some people start counting the hours right after a meal. Some prefer to wait an hour or two before counting, when the body has already digested the meal. This technique is most advisable for beginners so that they don't have a hard time adjusting to fasting techniques. Some people choose to extend this fast by skipping breakfast. Their first meal for the day is lunch, which also breaks their fasting period. Fasting is done twice a week. For the succeeding days, a person eats normally, at regular hours of breakfast, lunch and dinner.

During the fasting period, it is ideal not to eat any solid food. If going on long fasts, those that typically last for more than 12 hours, it is ok to drink liquids. These liquids are preferably water or clear soup. Avoid sugary drinks or those that contain large amounts of calories.

Also, during a fast, it is not advisable to engage in any moderate- to high-intensity type of activity. Doing so will not force the body to burn more fats. In fact, it will be placed on starvation mode, where in the body will refuse to give up its energy (fat) stores.

Hydration is very important when fasting. Drink lots of water in order to flush out toxins and any by-product or wastes produced by the processes stimulated by the fast. For instance, fasting promotes fat mobilization and burning. This process will produce free radicals and other wastes. To avoid these by-products from accumulating and adding more problems, promote its excretion by drinking lots of water.

During the non-fasting days, eat normally. This means eating a healthy, balanced meal. (I recommend 1500 to 1900 calories a day) It does not mean gorging on unhealthy foods or eating unlimited servings of healthy food. Always stay within healthy limits and avoid processed and other unhealthy foods like bad fats, proteins and carbs.

Conclusion

If you have read this book and are now ready to start implementing the changes I have suggested, then I wish you every success. I know that if you follow these guidelines and do what is written, you will be amazed how quickly your body will begin to change.

By the big day, you will not only look and feel terrific, but you will have healed your body in ways you never imagined possible.

This will set you on your way for a long, healthy and happy life that will continue long after you say the words "I do"

Congratulations and good luck, Melinda.

About the Author

Melinda (AKA Angela Frost) is an Amazon best selling author and..... health nut, tea lover, soapmaker cooking and freezing expert, crocheterer, and mom of three

Melinda loves anything to do with the home and the home life which is why she has taken her love and knowledge and turned them in a series of books called "The Home Life Series" In these books you will find recipes, crochet patterns, freezing tips, soap recipes, Holday recipes, Paleo and Diabetic cookbooks, smoothies, tea diets, and so much more.

She hopes you will enjoy them and that thery are able to help you in some way. And if so, please leave us a nice review, we would really appreciate it.

Melinda lives with her husband, 3 children 2 dogs, a cat, and a yellow bellied turtle in Swanville, Maine

Other Books in the "Home Life" Series by Melinda Rolf

101 DIY Household Hacks

The Flat Belly Tea Diet

The Two Week Diet and Detox Plan

The Wheat Belly Lifestyle

Prep Freeze Serve

Prep Freeze Serve Chicken

African Black Soap & How to Make It

How to Make Natural Handmade Soap

Loom Jewelry for Beginners

The Superfood Power Smoothie Book

Crockpot Recipes

Halloween

Meatless Eating

MELT Your Pain Away

The Raw Deal: Raw Food Lifestyle

Inside Crochet

Clean Eating

Planning the Perfect Christmas

Paleo Christmas

Paleo Thanksgiving

Mason Jar Recipes.

Mason Jar Gifts

Available at Amazon and other fine stores in e-book and paperback format

Made in the USA
Las Vegas, NV
02 February 2022

42875044R00039